CLOSE APART

Robert Cowan

Paloma Press 2018

Copyright © 2018 Robert Cowan

Book Design by C. Sophia Ibardaloza

Front Cover Image by Ada Cowan

ISBN-13: 978-1-7323025-0-1

Library of Congress Control Number: 2018942360

No part of this book may be reproduced or transmitted in any form or by any means, electronic or mechanical, including photocopying, recording, or by any information storage and retrieval system, without permission in writing from the author or publisher.

ALSO FROM PALOMA PRESS:

Blue by Wesley St. Jo & Remé Grefalda
Manhattan: An Archaeology by Eileen R. Tabios
Anne with an E & Me by Wesley St. Jo
Humors by Joel Chace
My Beauty is an Occupiable Space by Anne Gorrick & John Bloomberg-Rissman
peminology by Melinda Luisa de Jesús

PALOMA PRESS
Publishing Poetry+Prose with Panache since 2016
www.palomapress.net

for Ada

CONTENTS

CLOSE APART   9

    Hot and Black Out   11
    Relation Ships   13
    Gaslighting   14
    Understanding the Cuckoo   15
    People of Agape vs. State of Eros   16
    Do   17

CUENTOS DE ADA   19

    The Chrome-Toaster Stage   21
    Cheshire Cat   22
    Nella Nebbia   23
    Usual Life   24
    The Faerie Princesse   25
    Letting Go   26
    The Were-Fairy   27
    Tired from Silly School   28
    Fall   29
    She's   30
    The Ada C.   31
    New Holiday   32
    Worldviews   33

CLOSE CALL WITH SIBERIAN KICKBOXERS   35

    being deeply loved by someone   37
    can you cleanse your vision   38

think you're escaping	39
we walk through ourselves	41
be content with what you have	43
we mold clay into a pot	44
hold to the now	45

NOMINAL DETERMINISM 47

Sic Itur in Altum	49
Cowardice	51
1985	52
The Appellation of Careworn Bot	53
The Downhill Sailor Found Out	54
Primary Season	56

DON'T FORGET WHO WE MIGHT BE 59

DEMISNES 67

Time for Meaning	69
Uncertain Ends	71
The Assumption	72
Method and Truth	73
Effervescing and Effacing	75
Amaranthine Days	77

ABOUT THE AUTHOR 83

ACKNOWLEDGMENTS

Grateful acknowledgment is made to the editors of the following journals in which these pieces appeared, sometimes in slightly different form:

Bayou 50 (2008): "Cheshire Cat"

Green Spot Blue (7 Jan 2015): "Method and Truth"

Mayday 8 (Summer 2014): "Close Call with Siberian Kickboxers"

Mayday 12 (Winter 2018): "Amaranthine Days"

Thanks to Donna Masini and Tom Sleigh for their support. And deepest thanks to Ross Alvord, Denver Butson, Okla Elliott, Jennifer Hayashida, Jan Heller Levi, Lela Nargi, Matthew Silverman, and Shanti Thakur for their feedback on some or all of this manuscript, particularly Ashna Ali, Vanessa Baish, and David Rigsbee, whose help has been invaluable.

CLOSE APART

**Hot and Black Out
(August 14, 2003)**

When the southbound 6 train stops underground
it's dark blue for a long time. The chubby brown
girl across from me has an asthma attack, gasping

squeezed, as she lurches forward. Her mother is
silently hysterical, mumbling, sniveling in empty
space, as the girl wheezes painfully. Our still sweat

crystallizes in collective fear. Mercifully, a nurse
stumbles down with an inhaler and solace, as the
conductor commands us to trek through a tunnel

and climb up to street-level. In the light, thousands
are enervated ants. Mine is among the vast majority
of non-working cell phones. People have to walk

far in myriad directions and one woman bellows
into her phone, *An' I'm wearing those muthafuckin'
heels you gave me!* Most bars in Gramercy are

jammed with men in blue shirts drinking loudly and
spilling smoke onto the street. Slightly dazed from
the underground escape, I have a quick Belgian beer

at a brasserie open to the sidewalk on lower Park,
wondering whether my burstingly pregnant wife at
home in Brooklyn is ok, in this hot blackout. I walk

about 35 blocks, down to the first bridge, stopping
for a Gatorade in a shadowy, stifling bodega. There
is a long line and someone asks the Middle Eastern

proprietor, *Jou notice that people are walkin' outta
here wit stuff?* He shrugs—*Allah keeps tabs on those
people.* Did someone bring her the equivalent of an

inhaler or Gatorade? On the bridge, a tiny Asian
woman with her terrified young son is paralyzed,
clutching an iron girder, deathly afraid of both heights

and water. A towering West African guy and I have
to carry her over the bridge after she faints. On the
Southside of Williamsburg, it's like a Dominican

holiday—barbecue, loud merengue, children playing
soccer in the street. On North 7th, she's there—panic
to the side, having declined a glass of bad white wine

from Polish neighbors, slowly composing questions,
calmly straining, inhaling the stale industrial stillness
with an entreating look, awaiting me and the story

of my walk across such a trammeled Earth.

Relation Ships

My skiff floats over survival obligations
like vacuuming and picking up your library books
like mopping and getting you more *vinho verde*.

Your frigate looks so small from far away
its carriage-mounted guns no more discernible
than the various parts of the complex rigging.

My skiff bobs a little biliously as I approach you
knowing that the seas I have encountered thus far
today, no matter how rough, are nothing in comparison.

Your frigate looms so much larger now
the openings of its 32-pound cannons like black
holes emitting radiation into spacetime.

My skiff wishes, armed with this fore-knowledge, that
it hadn't heard on the radio today that most people
experience greater stress at home than they do at work.

Gaslighting

I showed you that one poem
and you said *you write well
but there's no there there.*

You saw that fuzzy animal dead
by the side of this road
like a peeled armadillo

and you said *there, there, little one.*
At that curiosity cabinet museum
was a pope holding aloft a crucifix

carved out of a grain of rice
you couldn't see through the magnifying
glass then a sudden glimpse

and you said *there! there it is!*
But now it's early November
and the car is so quiet and off-black

walls hug the road. I haven't started
moisturizing comprehensively and
my back itches, taut and dessicated

like the cracked leather seat, and
I imagine you here, scratching
and I say *there… ahh, there…*

thank you. But you're not here
you're there, with him, and
the road comes to a T and

the GAS light on the dash
flashes.

Understanding the Cuckoo

Sympathy for Éluard, cuckolded by Gala, with Dalí
from the Old French *cucault*, after *cucu*
which lays its eggs in another bird's nest.

How was he to compete
when he didn't have interns
to paint in his skies for him?

In Romance languages
they use the term for both
the bird and the adulterer,

but in English we've never
used cuckold
for the bird,

and it's hard to blame *la jolie russe*
for being bored with a tubercular
son of an accountant

when the Catalan peacock's
plumage so resembled
her own name

written on an ocean of sleep.

People of Agape v. State of Eros

His college-bound brother's friends
Nancy and Laurie chased him around
a soccer field on his 8th birthday

shrieking that he was was gonna be
a heartbreaker, their feathered blonde
and brown hair flowing, but he didn't

realize that they were talking about
teenage friendship, risking male friends
for female entanglement, only ever

having fallings-out with boys over girls
John punching him in the checker
-floored hallway over next-door Jill.

The guys understood the mating ritual
mechanincs though and got over
the injustices as quickly as the bloody

noses of their childhoods, like Mike
about Gothic Nicole by the golf course,
reforging bonds over skate boards

and sex pistols. Later though it was
the friendships with females that suffered
—when friends became lovers in dorm

rooms and dirty apartments and then exes
on both counts, although he didn't like
to name names, like Meg and Mai.

Thus he had eventually opted for
acquaintanceship over friendship
because there are other forms of hunger

just as there are other kinds of tribunals
based on publishing contracts and wind-
up toys and heart monitors.

Do

do you remember that time

Florida was close on the map and, when we got there, so far away
we got stoned on that Burgundy farm and you wanted *riento*
you threatened to punch that obnoxious Varanasi boy in the face
our old dog was a puppy who startled herself by farting
I got down on my knees by the wasteland waterfront

do remember that time

you conceded my mother meant well though you wanted to kill her
I danced to Prince on the pool table of that East Village dive
you quoted Laure while your cunt was in my mouth
or it will never have happened

do that time

you sang *Walkin' After Midnight* while the baby took a car-seat nap
you pretended to be Peter Falk trying to find his glasses
you didn't have to squirm before I licked your shoulder

do time

enough to satisfy our half-baked thirst for penance
before it does us

do

or all this will have passed

CUENTOS DE ADA

The Chrome-Toaster Stage

The first thing you said in the morning was
Shoes! Is that my pie? I want strawberry soup.
Eyes open. *We need to buy some more grapes.* Blink.
We were not even given a chance to recoup.

Then the chrome-toaster stage interrupted breakfast.
A palindrome of Lacan, you discovered no
lack of your expression in its '50s design,
etched across its side like a Maori logo.

Now you sink Pompeii with your own volcano.
Goggles on upside down, your hand at the ready,
anticipating the crater left by your calculated blow.
Vesuvius was never as you so steady.

As pumice and ash pelt, I lose the horizon.
Are you putting your next magnificent guise on?

Cheshire Cat

You distinguish between the ocean and the sea,
Proclaim yourself the captain-girl of mag-a-nets.
You inform me that yesterday we got married
And that you were the bride and I was the broom. It's

We, you claim, going on a trip called Brook-a-lyn,
That baking is always best done in the car, that
The door bit your thumb, and eyes are shaped like lemons—
Lines with a surprise, cow's-step elegance. I bet

You'll develop a taste for turnip cakes quite soon.
Your donkey, Lucy, will begin to walk herself.
You're probably planning a purple bead monsoon
And have a baby in your belly that's an elf.

As you learn and correct yourself, I lament the
Disappearance of each fantastic fabula.

Nella Nebbia

I drove you each morning from Sant'Arsenio
into the fog that mysteriously linked us
to daycare in Teggiano. You had just

turned one, we just three, listening to Björk
in the tiny rental Opel, the houses lurking
phantoms in various stages of reconstruction

after the earthquake twenty-four years ago,
Berlusconi's government having done even
less than the previous to provide relief.

Fellini-esque faces streak by like Bacon
portraits reminding us why our families left
these craggy hill towns a century ago.

You admire the tiny hundreds of this Saint
Arsenio in niches in crumbling walls with little
glass doors and fake flowers, but your impeccable

brow furrows, knowing these implicit memories,
like those of our ancestors, will be lost to childhood
amnesia.

Usual Life

Our old neighbor did a jig last night, smiling,
with jazz-hands twinkling, as he told me he
had raped you the other day. I leapt out

of the dream, gasping, for you are only three-
years-old. But you know how to comfort me,
you who've chosen us as your Bowie kooks,

you who warn me not to *step in the slosh*
for fear my feet would get wet and cold, you who
tell me your cuentos de Ada, who explain

that this is *usual life: buildings on the ground,
and balloons with people holding them,
wheels on the ground*,

you who assure me that you are writing
in a magazine to show us that
everything is really real.

The Faerie Princesse

A fairy in Latino neighborhood stories.
From beyond the Bosporus, she is an island.
In Hindi, she always measures half the saris.
A precursor to happiness in the Highlands.

In Tibet, her brother tells tales of her silence.
Across Russian steppes, Adachka will move the gears.
Two feet tall, with a bold wispy-haired transcience,
One eye slightly more open, cool sleek grin, and ears.

The wings invisible—are they singles or pairs?
By comparison, tinker with nymph, sylph, dryad,
On shiny planets, you'll find but manticore snares,
On muddy pallets or in the Chinese Triad,

On North Seventh Street, fooled out a Barnum egress,
Ethereal, you won't find the Faerie Princesse.

Letting Go

Today the faerie said goodbye with conviction,
Just as we had known it was likely to begin.
She mounted her yellow spotted giraffe fiction,
Her purple shoes held aloft on parallel shins.

She gave us an eerie look that transcends most kin
That could only mean, *I have something in my pants*,
But we knew that this act would be the final rinse.
Knew where she was headed, without a backward glance.

All preceding evasiveness to her parents
Became clear in this one moment misbegotten.
Can't remember a time with such ominous tints.
We were inert, dumbstruck. She haughty and rotten.

She was hitting the road again, not unawares.
Now if we would just, please, carry her down the stairs.

The Were-Fairy

You roam the backyards of Victorian London—
the night sprite of the black rose,
under moonshine you morph,

from cherubic grin to hellion sneer,
thorns burst from beneath your porcelain lobes
and mockingbirds scatter at your daemonic grunts,

your slippers elongate and curl, sleeves
become hairy gauntlets, your gown
inks, and bat-wings shred your milk skin,

your limbs take on the sardonic lilt of vines
and until the crepuscule of dawn you tend your rosebed.
Yet we find you in the morning sunrays

sprawled sideways, covers liberally strewn about,
unaware of your scarlet secret.

Tired from Silly School

She put on
her neat goon
and got into bad.

Deep slop would feel
so lively after
such a full whack.

Would she dream
of fair ease or have
more neat mares?

Fall

The girl is dark
around the eyes,
sullen about a friend

who has wronged her,
but I don't know how
to tell her that the planet

operates on such
moments of tension
because she would

only believe it if
she heard it from
a tree.

She's

my glass turtle because
there's beach glass
stick because stick

bugs are people purple
cloud wine drinker
although it's actually

apple berry cherry
juice, water spiller
(happens)

ant queen
water castle
sky beetle

because it's
all so simple
so Baroque,

until you have
the permanent thigh
bruise of the middle

aged woman,
and beyond.

The Ada C.

You had a Nietzsche doll.
You played with the gray-
clad classicist and cared

for his fragility, breastfed
him and dragged him around
by his moustache. When we

got in the car, we'd say,
Don't forget Nietzsche, honey.
But Nietzsche was not from

your planet—New Kentucky,
and you didn't understand why
he thought you were so funny,

so under sinewy sycamores,
wrinkled in the lamplight,
you suggested he go to sleep.

New Holiday

You can put all
the pieces of paper
that you write

about me
into a book
and call it *Ada Rob*

and give it to me
as a present
for Daughter's Day.

Worldviews

papa, did you know
that drinks have wrinkles
when you blow

papa, the sun is pushing the wind
into our country and the wind
is pushing the sun into another country

papa, when you make up
a beautiful song does water
come out of your eyes

CLOSE CALL WITH SIBERIAN KICKBOXERS

**being deeply loved by someone gives you strength,
while loving someone deeply gives you courage**

The taciturn kick-boxers and I are exhausting the path of light through the trees, careening down a crevasse of road carved through remarkably straight conifers, when a full black vehicle much larger than our aluminum can charges us directly until we all come to a blinding halt, halogen antlers interlocked. Four men leap out of the car yelling, dressed in full riot-gear and with pistols, what I think are Kalashnikovs, and stammering footsteps demand we exit our vehicle. My insides twist. The three kick-boxers tell me not to say anything. We climb out cautiously, hands up. They make us put them on the car roof, spread our legs, and frisk us by running the cold machine gun barrels up the insides of our bare legs, still hot from the sauna. I assume that they are police, forgetting that this is Yeltsin's Russia, not the Soviet Union.

I had just finished college and was avoiding responsibility. It was during the first of the big bank scandals; people were losing their life savings and no one was getting paid. This area, a couple hours north of the Kazakh border, just beyond the Urals, the beginning of Siberia, is run by the mafia. Why had I thought coming here—to work at an orphanage, of all things—was a good idea? Not that I thought that all the men at the camp were connected with the mafia. Most of them were ostensibly unemployed coaches, though some had shady ties to the Honda Civic-driving toughs in Kamensk-Uralskiy, a small city once known for its cannon works, where the orphanage was. The children were out of school, so the orphanage was emptied, and they had been sent to this summer camp in the woods, populated mostly by children who have families and would make fun of them. There was a pool, filled with water from the radioactive river nearby, and a music teacher with an accordion. The three sports they could play were chess, soccer, and kick-boxing. It was summer, so the sky got dark around 11:00 and light again around 3:00, but under the trees the darkness lingered for longer.

Druzhba ("Friendship") was an old scout camp from the Soviet era, with a statue of Lenin and slogans about what "pioneer" children—as boy- and girl-scouts are called in Russian—should do to support the system. But my kids, from the Sinarski Children's Home, were not pioneers of any sort. They were not forging new territory. They were more like the kick-boxers—but ones with poor balance, thrown on their backs, kicking and punching with all they had just to get up. Turtle kick-boxers. For children in Russian orphanages are like cases in Dickens novels. The only "toys" at Sinarski, which housed over two hundred kids, were one bicycle with no seat or chain and a pile of aerosol cans. I was responsible for 14 kids, between the ages of eight and 14, 24-hours-a-day, for three months. Two of mine had witnessed one of their parents murdering the other parent. One beautiful boy, Vanya, would run in a circle for 45 minutes at a time, laughing his head off. It was funny, and terrible. But after he broke into the electrician's dacha, he was sent away. To somewhere worse.

At night, I would retreat to my room and read the two books I'd brought: the *Tao Te Ching* and *Ulysses*—one a self-help manual for a king, the other a compendium of obstacles to orgasm—both comforting in their ways. Both with something to teach me about fate.

can you cleanse your vision till there is no blemish?

I was supposed to be working with three other Americans—two women and another man—but, as it worked out, I was alone. The other guy, Michael, was one of the most singularly amoral people I've ever met. We'd bonded on the plane over a common interest in melancholic British pop music, he a lumbering, affable guy with a Master's in Russian. The children loved him immediately. He was recently married, but fooled around with a girl who worked at the camp his first night there. She was about 17. Then he leveled with me that he didn't care about the children and had only applied to the program to get a visa. He had a job interview in St. Petersburg and when he left, he lied to everyone at the camp that he would be back in a week. They believed him at first. I knew he would not return. I did, however, see him again, years later, on West 57th Street. Michael went ashen as I called his name. He was with the wife he'd betrayed that first night in Siberia and in the intervening period had gone to, perhaps unsurprisingly, law school.

Melinda and Serena, the two women, had mercifully been sent to a camp ten miles away. They were Mormons who did not drink, smoke, ingest caffeine, or take part in any fun that could remotely be construed as illicit. The Russians thought they were from Mars. I thought they were from Hell. They turned out to be from Spokane. They had brought three books with them: *The Book of Mormon* in English, *The Book of Mormon* in Russian, and *Jane Eyre*. In their light, I preferred Michael and Joyce's Leopold Bloom. At least they appeared to enjoy life.

think you're escaping and run into yourself. longest way round is the shortest way home

I somehow managed to get away from everyone one day when I was feeling overwhelmed and take a walk on the path along the river through the forest of birches. There was a tree fallen across the path, suspended so that one had to duck under it to proceed. I was deep in thought—trying to decide whether I too would abandon this volunteer work, which was turning out to be more than I bargained for—but stopped, feeling eyes on me. An owl no fewer than eighteen inches high was sitting right before me on the fallen tree, about fifteen feet away. An animal maybe fifty yards off broke a branch on the ground, and the owl swiveled in surveillance, forth and back. I was frozen, the two of us in silence, opposites: I motionless but breathing audibly and it turning like a noiseless glockenspiel. The far-off sounds faded and the owl finally came to rest its stare on me for seconds that seemed like excruciating, fascinating minutes, as if my ears were covered and my eyes as large as its discs. Then, it spread wings of four or five feet across and with a single, suddenly loud, rustled beat flew past me, leaving a dark empty space amidst the white birch stripes, and an eerie breeze.

This had been quite the opposite of a night in the forest the following week, when I'd dealt with the stress of being there differently. I'd gotten terribly drunk with the camp staff, which consisted mostly of people who worked at the camp in summer but who, during the year in Kamensk, were normally nurses, janitors, cafeteria workers, and from that enormous professional class the Soviets called "engineers." Drinking vodka with them on other nights, I had found myself forced to be strategic about rationing food so that I could make it to the bottom of the bottle. Following their lead, I would take a big whiff of black bread before downing my shot. I would take every piece of chocolate or *shashlik* offered. But when you triumphantly reach the end of that bottle, suddenly a full one emerges from under the table, and you realize, glancing down, that there are six more on the floor. On this particular night, in a clearing, around a big fire, we had danced and laughed—a lot of jokes about hedgehogs, the humor of which was lost on me. A fat nurse in her fifties, with gold teeth and curly hair in an unnatural orange peeking out from under her kerchief, had gotten down on her knees amidst cajoling and hoots and proposed marriage to me on the condition that I took her back to America.

I don't know how I made it back to my room, but I was poked awake by sunlight and the giggling of a crowd of children perpendicular to my gaze, as I lay face-down on the steps up to my door, thankfully not quite in the vomit I'd indecorously deposited alongside them.

we walk through ourselves, meeting robbers, ghosts, giants, old men, young men, wives, widows, brothers-in-love. but always meeting ourselves

The day I had the machine gun in my crotch, it was 91° and we were coming back from the farm in Mermansk that belonged to one of the kick-boxers' parents—the one who hadn't even the courtesy to grunt and who looked like he had been carved out of tooth enamel with a dirty, blunt instrument.

We were all sore from a barefoot soccer game earlier in the day. Not everyone who worked at the camp had sport shoes, so, to be fair, no one wore them. This I was used to by then. What hurt was that the stocky, thickly muscled maintenance guy had nailed me with his shins of steel, and I was still hobbling a bit. He was covered in jet hair from his furry toes to his Windex-blue eyes—one of the strange Eurasian looks of Siberia. My friend Genya took him out for me later in the game, laughing. Genya was a martial arts enthusiast and a veteran of the war in Afghanistan, who'd come home at age 19 so disturbed that he'd attempted to commit *seppuku* with a sword. The astonishingly long, deep, twisted scars on his abdomen quaked with laughter as he celebrated his takedown.

One of the kick-boxing coaches, Volodya, had said the silent kick-boxer was from a farm down the road where they had a sauna. So we had smoked some stinky Kazakh weed after the game and driven out there in Volodya's half-cylinder car. I was a little apprehensive since I had heard gunfire out that way a few days before and the swimming instructor's wife had been murdered by the mafia in Kamensk (as a message to her brother) and he had not dared to go into the city for her funeral.

The farm was actually a little outside Mermansk, which was itself only a crossroads marked with three Siberian houses—dark brown with the elaborate blue and white window casings. The quiet pedi-pugilist's mother had given us milk directly from their cow and some radishes, while her son stoked the fire in the "sauna." We filed into his room, which had newspapers nailed to the walls—to cut down on the wind from across the plain, I guess—and a large glass cabinet with about 40 bottles of local vodka and several thousand flies. The so-called sauna consisted of a small set of planks that he had constructed around an old iron furnace hull, which he filled with wood and set alight. It got so hot in there that we had to wear hats so that our ears wouldn't blister. We went in two at a time—the silent one and Volodya, and me and the fourth one of us, the young guy. The young kick-boxer didn't seem to have only kick-boxing going for him. He was handsome and muscular, with more on the ball mentally than the other two, or so it had seemed in the couple weeks I'd seen him around with Masha, a trampy girl I'd wanted to sleep with, who wasn't his girlfriend either. I'd stayed away from her though, for it seemed likely that I could get hurt by someone for making overtures to her.

As I entered the sauna, I hit a moistureless wall and I struggled to figure out whether I'd die faster breathing in the pure heat or not breathing at all. But, Mitya (I think the young guy's name was Dimitri) pushed me in and before I had any time to strain my eyes and lungs open, much less acclimate, he began brutally beating my shocked body with leafy birch branches. I was surprised to find that this was masochistically soothing and, for reasons that I didn't entirely understand, took no small pleasure in beating him back. We stayed in as long as endurance allowed—about four minutes—and then let the real masochists back in.

Afterwards, we walked around the farm a little, eating bitter salted cucumbers from the silent one's silent mother's garden—a silence uninterrupted by gunfire. Twilight seemed far away, off across the steppe, but we knew that beneath the birches and pines it was already night.

be content with what you have; rejoice in the way things are/when you realize there is nothing lacking, the whole world belongs to you

I got one day off that whole summer, which I spent curled up in a ball on Zoya's couch in Kamensk, the victim of intestinal mutiny. I had been so careful not to drink any unboiled water. I'd gotten used to drinking immersion-coil-heated Nescafé in the scorch of summer. But the night before, Zoya, the sexagenarian English teacher who was working at the camp, had brought me back to her apartment in the city so that I could meet her children and their spouses, and drink—a lot.

Before they all arrived, she and I watched a game show on which three carpenters used axes, their traditional tool, in various competitions: making as thin and long a shaving as possible from a long plank, hammering in a giant nail through a beefsteak tomato as deeply as possible without injuring the tomato. The winner, after demonstrating not inconsiderable skill, won a boom box, the runner-up (no joke) cans of beans.

Hours later, after many swigs of vodka and much conversation about everyone's lack of money, Zoya brought out a tray with small glasses of water on it and I was so parched that I greedily downed two. Months later, my gastroenterologist in New York said I had the worst stool test results he had ever seen—bacillary dysentery, giardia, and two other kinds of parasites I don't remember the names of. He gave me two courses of the highest dose of flagyll he'd ever given, a drug that kills just about every living thing in one's body. I had diarrhea for the next month after that night at Zoya's, getting to know well the camp's white-washed toilet hut, an enclosed platform with a hole in it, that the children jokingly called Bely Dom, "the White House."

My gastro-intestinal tract finally evened out seven years later.

we mold clay into a pot, but it is the emptiness inside that makes the vessel useful

The children would be particularly rambunctious when it was time to put them to bed. Once, histrionic, 11-year-old Kolya was standing on top of a dresser introducing a dance routine two of the girls were to do by announcing, arms outstretched: "Paramount Pictures presents…!"—the only English words I'd heard him say all summer. Kolya was the youngest of four Uzbek kids at Sinarski who had the same mom and four different dads, so each with a slightly different skin-tone. Kolya was the darkest and thus the most picked on. He was my unofficial Sancho Panza, the one who dreaded most the day I was to leave. I was told only the week, not the day or time, they were to come for me.

The day they came, the children were in the middle of a variety show the whole camp had put together. The announcement came over the loudspeaker—the one that had woken me up in the morning with songs like "Purple Rain" and "Jailhouse Rock"—that Robert was leaving. The performance ended in a vocal explosion—audience and performers alike—running, screaming at me, and out of the hall. As I dashed back to my dacha to throw together my few things, a crowd of at least a hundred children—not just my 14, but all the others at the camp I'd played with and known—mobbed me. Most of them burst into tears: "Don't leave us! Don't leave us, Robert!" In the midst of all this, Vera

Nikolaevna, a woman I had worked with closely, begged me out of nowhere to take her with me, sobbing. As I climbed aboard the small bus that had rolled up, the children shook it, screaming and bawling.

It was arranged that I would spend two days relaxing at a sanatorium in Kamensk, unfortunately with the Mormons. I would stare out over broken Kamensk for two days and say almost nothing to them. I turned to my Lao-Tzu and Joyce on the bedside table, but they were as silent as the kick-boxer's mother on the farm.

hold to the now, the here, through which all future plunges to the past

At the sanatorium, my mind drifted back to that day that I'd had the Kalashnikov in my back, a moment in which my ears were not filled with laughter or even sobs, but with frantic shouting, extinguishing the images of the children, the owl, the pragmatically romantic nurse in the forest. I had nothing on me except my room key on a string around my neck, and my clothes were distinctly un-First-World in origin, so I wasn't worried about being robbed or found out. And yet, we had heard of random people around there being shot for no particular reason.

But then, out of the somber gloaming of the road through the forest a third vehicle careered to a screech and men in more professional looking outfits began screaming at our menacing friskers. The Kalashnikov-wielders darted into their car and toward the light between the trees down-road, the M16-handling "professionals" in immediate pursuit. Almost before I could turn around, we were free to go, dramatically unmolested, not entirely sure what had just happened.

The prospects for the kids at the Sinarski Children's Home were not promising. Over twenty years later and with a teenage girl now myself, I know that most of the girls either became prostitutes or went to work in the remaining factories in Kamensk or are unemployed at the jobs they may have trained for. The boys are probably marginally employed, rich gangsters, in prison, or dead, unless they fled for the oil and gas fields. My mother has sent Zoya money for operations for uterine cancer.

Having finally wrestled the children into bed that night, I stumbled back to my own room, trying to decide whether to read Lao-Tzu or Joyce. What light would they shed on the fact that I had so easily escaped one of the gruesome fates that so many come to here? Muscles sore from soccer, my skin smooth from the sauna, I didn't read at all. I lay staring at the cracks in the dacha ceiling, listening to the machine gunfire down the road.

NOMINAL DETERMINISM

Sic Iter in Altum

Robert   I am not Robert Walser, although I will spend the remainder of my days in a sanatorium. I am not Robert Schumann, although a hand injury

will end all my dreams. I am not Robert Deniro, but I have been a guerilla heating engineer. I am not Robert Plant, despite having carried girls around

like human vacuum-cleaners. I am not Rob Lowe, but I am a young blood. I am not Bob Hope, Bob Dylan, Bobbie Kennedy, Browning, Burns, Frost,

Bruce   Rossellini, or E. Lee, but Robbie, Robber-Dobber, Bob, Bobby, Bobert, **Роберт**, Rabbit—all from the Old High German *Hruod-berht*, "fame-bright."

Nor am I a Bruce. They came from the Norman lands now called Brix, situated between Cherbourg and Valognes, and the surname comes from *de Bruis*.

Robert the Bruce was crowned the first king of Scotland in 1306. His heart and the rest of his body are interred in separate abbeys, just as he is only

Cowan   my namesake—Bruce in spirit, not in letter— separated in heart and mind, like the channel between the Continental and the Analytic.

I am, though, a Cowan. The name, widespread in Scotland and Ulster, is an Anglicized form of the old Gaelic *MacEoghain* or *MacEoin*. The Gaelic

prefix "mac" (meaning "son of") plus the personal name *Eoghan* from the old Celtic *Oue(i)n*, but believed to derive ultimately from the Greek

Ph.D. *Eugenious*—"born lucky" or "well-born."
Our motto is "This is the way to heaven,"
but the analytics show few followers.

We can't differentiate ourselves, though, by saying
what we are or are not—a figurative Bruce, a literal
Cowan, any Robert, a doctor to philosophers, a

lucky-born fame-bright son of competing lands—like
an alien coming to America and expecting acceptance
by saying his name is George Quincy Jefferson.

Cowardice

When we were 13, Tommy and I took the
bus to White Plains and talked with an
elderly woman who was hard of hearing
and eventually asked our names.

Tom Rose.
Oh, rose. How pretty! And you, young man?
Robbie Cowan.
Coward?! Coward?! Like the shoes?!

I had never heard of such shoes,
but she had
inadvertently, imperceptibly, egregiously
cut me.

Cowardice was not an association
I sought, Tom teased me for
weeks, and it would ring in
my spleen for years,

but today I feel
brave, bold, intrepid
(not all the time, but now)
as I say that

I hope
—inappropriately and uncharitably—
that that
old bitch is dead.

1985

Caught between the Roald Dahl my father gave me,
the Eleanor Roosevelt my mother admired, and my own
grating Suicidal Tendencies, striving to become a nebulous ideal

invented by a romantic student in his garret.
Avoiding artistic commitment, ideological stance,
necessary repetition. Failing to allow oneself failure.

You can give up on yourself because you don't know
what to say, evading selves out of which you might have grown,
willingly letting possibilities boil off due to the incessant droning

of inertia or duty, creating one's own dystopia out of soccer
practice and mescaline. Remember who you might better
have been. I, for example, know that I am unlikely

to ever give up on espresso or whiskey, that the limit
of my maturity was achieved at age 14, when I decided,
based on *Annie Hall*, that I wanted to be a New York

intellectual—a species in purgatory. But, as Beatrice said to him,
From fear and from shame I wish that you henceforth divest
yourself, so that you may no more speak like one who is dreaming.

The Appellation of Careworn Bot[*]
by Baron Towcer

He wore the browner coat so it wouldn't be stained by the
    browner taco,
walked down the beta cornrow to the rote cow barn and found
    the crowbar note.

It said, *Crower to Nab Cort Rawbone*, but he didn't have time
    to enact,
borrow the cento barrow from Tor Cowbarne,

who had gone to the recrown at Bo with the Towbar Crone.
So, he took the crowner boat to do some Towbar recon.

He found the crower at Nob, with his crower baton.
But "no boar net crow," as they say, so now he's known as
    Careworn Bot.

---

[*] The Appellation of Robert Cowan
by Robert Cowan
(Transposition by Berto Wranco)

He wore the robert cowan so it wouldn't be stained by the robert cowan,
walked down the robert cowan to the robert cowan and found the robert cowan.

It said, Robert Cowan Robert Cowan, but he didn't have time to robert
cowan the robert cowan from Robert Cowan,

who had gone to the robert Cowan with the Robert Cowan.
So, he took the robert cowan to do some Robert cowan.

He found the Robert at Cowan, with his robert cowan.
But "no robert cowan," as they say, so now he's known as Robert Cowan.

The Downhill Sailor Found Out

The painting was large—about
4'x5'—mostly black, with a
giant sweeping white and blue

bird in the upper left and a dinky
orange boat descending at a
steep angle in the lower right.

Invisible to the viewer was the
Downhill Sailor and somehow
he had been found out. Found

to be going downhill, which
defies the laws of the sea. Found
to be sailing, which flouts

the rules of landlubbing. Found
to be untalented, to be unsmart,
to not speak other languages, not

know his history. Found to have
been bad at hanging out, to not
know where he was going. But

it may not matter whether he
was an imposter, for perhaps,
perhaps he wasn't the Downhill

Sailor. Maybe we couldn't see
him in the boat because he
wasn't there; maybe he was the

giant blue-white bird, sweeping
across the sea, looking down on
that boat and at us in it. Of

course, we can't know now
now that the painting is gone,
put out at the curb.

Primary Season

Ted Kennedy: *So, why have you hated my family so much?*

Jello Biafra: *I don't hate your family.*

TK: *But why have you been so disrespectful to us?*

JB: *Because it's punk. We satirize hyprocrisy, if we're doing it right. You're symbols, not people.*

TK: *Are you not a symbol?*

JB: *Of course, I am.*

TK: *Of what?*

JB: *Decay, fragmentation... entrepreneurship. I'm quintessentially Californian. That's the irony of punk starting in New York. It's much better suited to California. We're more moralistic and we're not bound by the same lame social rules.*

TK: *Hmm. I guess... But do you feel bad about calling your band "Dead Kennedys" now that most of us are actually dead?*

JB: *Why would I?*

TK: *Because death demands respect.*

JB: *No. Nature demands respect. Death is just a part of its cycles.*

TK: *Fine. [Sighs.] So then, who will you be voting for in the primaries?*

JB: *Death. Or Bernie Sanders.*

TK: *Can I ask you... do you feel that I did ok, as a politician, in representing those who are underrepresented?*

JB: *Yeah, you did pretty well. You do know, right, that I choose your family because they were symbols of American glam, not because your politics were particularly objectionable? Obviously, there were far more disturbing political families out there. They just weren't as beautiful as your family.*

TK: *Yes, I get that. But, so you really think I did ok? 'Cause I wasn't actually my family's first choice to be a successful career politician.*

JB: *I know. That must have been hard for you. And I'm sorry about your losing so many family members. I lost my only sister about 15 years ago....*

TK: *I'm sorry to hear that. Can I ask you, what's your real name?*

JB: *Boucher. Eric Boucher.*

TK: *As in French for "butcher"?*

JB: *Yup.*

DON'T FORGET WHO WE MIGHT BE

for Ross

The top log burns so brightly, with such contrast;
the lower logs, to whom it owes its flames,
smolder—dulled—less dramatic.
The young shine on the shoulders of the old,

for thousands of years falling asleep comforted
by the ancient light and the heat of Promethean fire,
rocking a wooden chair. The brick and slate of the
fireplace are foundational, the slab of rock is first

or the browed sheer cliff faces, structures built upward
from horizontal stone or pulled sideways out of verticality,
cities carved in relief or constructed rock by rock,
on a time-plane of subtly shifting red gray and ochre concepts.

The World Trade Center was screwed right into the bedrock,
silver helix columns twisting like steel DNA through formed
    strata,
he unsure whether they had come up out of the earth
or been placed down into it, imagining their vast majorities

below the surface with but short final lengths visible.
The holes they dug for those shafts were the play
of titan children digging to China—so deep, so wide across,
the holes became their own entities—giant phenomenal
    nothings.

The pentagon below 14th Street became the nut speared
by twin screws, like the raspberries his nephew
wore on his thumbs, but these were black holes,
vacancies so massive, absences so glaring

that it seemed the city would be sucked down into them,
vacuum holes vying for supremacy—Madison Square Garden
sucked down one, the Morgan Library down the other,
leviathan mouths, arguing maws of a Bronx Roc

and a Staten Island Gamera wearing white tank-tops:
"Oh, *yeah*?! Fuck *me*?!! Fuck *meee*?!!! Fuuuck *meeeee*??!!!"
—neck-vein-popping— "Fuuuuuuck. *Yoooooou*!!!!"
He saw the army of ants dig on rainy days,

drains for the glaciers of the Hudson Valley
melting and washing down all they had carved out,
rushing down gigantic iron grates into the mammoth
sewer system of the world. The worker-ants left

to contend with the glacial erratics, immovable crumbs,
the soil terribly labor-intensive to cultivate; cotton
ants that long ago formed the rock walls that cover
the region, like the strings of vertebrae he'd walked

sectioning the Aran Islands, the isles themselves
slabs of rock risen out of the ocean.
There is a rock formation there, on Inishmaan,
called "Synge's Chair"—a spot looking East out

onto the Atlantic—from which the playwright composed,
writing from a seat that fills in potholes and shores
up foundations built on specious puns.
It's poor feng-shui to build a city at the bottom of a valley,

where the wind rushes down unobstructed and whips
through the canyons of buildings, sculpting the denizens
into sand people. But walking avenue North,
a giant U of wind nearly knocking him off his feet,

he appreciated the culmination of the country in the city.
As a boy, he'd seen the New York Cosmos destroy
Team America and had gloated over it;
studying in Europe during the first Bush league,

he had introduced himself as a New Yorker first,
American only reluctantly afterward, keeping in mind
a quote he'd incorrectly attributed to Mark Twain:
"New York is an island between Europe and America."

While he'd eventually mellowed on that distinction,
the difference between television and live action on
9/11 re-established the gulf between New York City
and America for a while. The smoke and steam escapes

the end of the log and its hurling nature is intermittently
interrupted by the flames on its back.
He'd grown up in the absurd idyll of Sunnyside
Avenue in Pleasantville between the Goodmans

and the Roses. Among other immediate neighbors,
Mr. Glynn: A Boo Radley-type widower,
at least to the children; Gunther Silverman:
whose heart only functioned at 15%, but at a much

higher percentage metaphorically; The Trumans,
who moved to Nairobi; The Aldens: he grim ex-Navy,
she always smiley. There were the Korins from Argentina;
the Roman family with the giant German Shepherd;

Esther from Morocco; and the four Nguyen kids
(Tuan, Hoai, Hahn, Thuan), the fifth in his mother's
belly, to be born here (David). Gunther and Dave
both gone in their 30s, as are most of those families on the street.

Some kids had overdetermined names, a set-up.
There was a Medea born to a couple in his college dorm.
And a kid in his present neighborhood called Faust.
There were the Anglo names that got ruined by natural

occurrences that got anthropomorphized: Sandy, Irene, Charlie…
And human occurrences that got animalized: Adolf, Idi, Osama…
They'd fallen as adults. Had they fallen as children,
letting out a huge scream and then being quiet

while taking a massive inhale, the anticipation of the second
even louder shriller scream that would be so much worse—
that scintilla of anticipation just excruciating—
the scream that now makes him feel such profound

sympathy for both child and parent? Relieved his child
is way past that, on to lipstick and nail polish.
As a boy, he'd hated all the girls' chipped and ragged nail polish.
He wanted them to remove all of it.

His mother seemed to be doing her nails all the time—
all twenty of them in bright red. To the point that
her nails were yellow without polish on them.
But he didn't want the girls to wear polish at all

if it was just going to get destroyed immediately.
Wait till you're older—already avuncular—
don't grow up too fast. But now, grown up
too fast, asking how he will damage his own child:

Is there, as Will Self asserted, a quantity theory—
or rather practice—of insanity? If they were four or six,
would there be the same amount of dysfunction
more evenly distributed, than between three?

Finally, the bark separates and it all erupts into dancing flame;
then the log finally gives, falls, and the whole enterprise shifts.
That one year, they had shared the number 121—
his classroom number, his stepbrother's school bus number,

his stepmother's classroom number. Are such affinities chance?
How does one remember who one is? Perhaps it is to be found
in the translations between brain, hands, and heart—1-2-1.
Work area code: 212. Home zip code: 11231. Not binary,
    though.

Wasn't a zero required to make sure the programs didn't crash?
How do we know the code is correct? Have people done
what they say they did? Is the language with which they
describe their life-acts accurate? Are they put, by themselves

or their biographers, in terms that romanticize them?
When we mix mythology and biography, we get either
biology or mythography, but probably not both.
The only famous person from his hometown was Allen See

—otherwise known as Gavin McLeod, or Captain Stubing—
until Tommy Hilfiger and Ace Frehley moved in,
the latter crashing his car into the 7-Eleven upon arrival.
In the mall, in the antique store, they would turn to each

other and say, "Don't forget who we are." Don't forget
that we are warriors—our alignment chaotic neutral,
armor class high, with many hit points. Don't forget
our high marks for strength, intelligence, wisdom,

dexterity, constitution, and charisma. Don't forget that
we can create ourselves in whatever mold we choose.
His character class: barbarian magic-user.
Out the window, the woods are dark but the sky still
    blackening,

the branch extremities overhead creating curved biometries.
This is the spot, up here in the mountains—no landline,
cell service, internet, cable—just fireplace, whiskey, and
snow falling on hermetically sealed deer. Whenever they said,

"Let's get outta here" in a movie, he imagined coming here.
And yet he worried that he'd hear someone's tires
compress-crunching the snow outside, ruining everything,
for he knew that we will need this wooden rocking chair

on the eve of post-life, just as we needed rocking in the womb.

DEMISNES

Time for Meaning

Lois and Mark's dog died. I had wondered
who would be the third: Harold Pinter,
Eartha Kitt, and now Jakey. What did they

have in common other than dying within a
few days of each other? Eartha was hardly
Pinteresque and Pinter unlikely to have been

Earthalike. I didn't even know Jakey. But
now their three strands are bound together.
What happens when people born far apart in

time and space die almost simultaneously?
Rudolf Nureyev and Dizzy Gillespie died on
January 6th, 1993. Gerry Mulligan and Gene

Kelly died within two weeks of each other in
1996. I first knew Gerry Mulligan from his
recording of "I Got Rhythm" and I first

knew Gene Kelly from *An American in
Paris*, in which he sings that song playing
a character named Jerry Mulligan. But why

did I think that River Phoenix and Mother
Theresa died in the same week? I know
that one of them collapsed outside

The Viper Room. What does it mean that I
share my own birthday with the discoverer
of Saturn's rings (1629), an interim

president of the Republic of Texas (1788),
the head of the Lubavitcher Jews (1902),
"Papa Doc" Duvalier (1907), Frank Serpico

(1936), and a Czech porn star that reminds me
of my wife (1975)? What time was
everybody else born? Did they leave loose

ends? Were they greeted with loose
beginnings? Who will die on the day I die?
Dick Cheney? Jack Black? Our rabbit? It's

ok. I won't have a lot to do that day, for
people pass in and out of the world and we
attempt to tether them to numbers—our

Hindu-Arabic numerals, the sexigesimal
system of minutes we got from the
Sumerians. But now archeologists think that

Christ was born around 3 B.C., so the rope
has become unstayed from the anchor of
years anyway.

Uncertain Ends

Elegies can be potentially about
the way he ran pigeon-toed
through Ralph's, how they always

hated gift-giving on a schedule,
how she blinked for so much
longer than everyone else.

Possible eulogies might conclude
that she really just wanted
a Stickley coffee table, that he

fought hard for deaf rights,
that the twins knew they
would die together too.

Unlikely epitaphs include:
*Devoted husband, loving father,
deluded minstrel. This ornate*

*box is too full of chemicals to
decompose. Plots of land serve
the human need to conquer.*

Maybe memories question why
he slept with other women, whether
she purposely knocked the oak board

onto the kitten, the fact that Mom's
tics are now mine, why we speak of
re-birth instead of re-death.

The Assumption

I've often assumed I would commit suicide
in my sixties, when my child is grown
and my parents are dead, like Hemingway;

he was 68. There is a photo of him from around
then, in a plaid shirt and a tweed cap kicking
a tin can down a road—my favorite work

of his. Then my parents died suddenly
in the same month and the bombardment
of support so pulverized my ego that I felt

ungrateful at ever having had such visions.
Let's see, though, how I feel if I make it
to Hemingway's sixties, for, when I am

honestly silent, I remember that someone wrote
that the suicidal tendency belies a murderous
impulse, and they have got me there. Murder

is toward the top of my bucket list, but not
till I'm older, when I am ready to fully lose
myself and hurt those around me less,

for extreme experience must be isolated to be
effective, to approach stark divinity.

Method and Truth
Sean Flaherty (1966-2015)

Initially I was skeptical about your method:
minimal revision, as if a Romantic muse
really did breathe inspiration into you.

My training made me suspect.
Initially, you didn't try to publish them,
just emailed them to everyone you knew

in true *samizdat* fashion. I loved that,
but then you found other venues
that embraced our public poetry

and you published 97 poems about your cancer,
your magnum opus: *The Doctor Series*.
Somehow, I spent your last full night on Earth

with you in the hospice center at Bellevue,
a center of sanity in a hospital for the crazy.
How it was me, I don't know, I whose

earnestness you respected and surely mocked.
I was out of words by that point, and read
to you all the things people were writing

about you on your Facebook wall, although
many were people you couldn't stand, I'm sure.
We seemed to have reached the point at which

words utterly failed to capture sensation and I
didn't know how to express the ineffable,
now that your bright spots had become so blue.

And your method clicked a sense switch—
it did not need major revision, only
checks for tact and emotional accuracy,

because those unspoken hermeneutics revealed
that you lit up this crooked joint by making love
to the absurdity of existence, Sean.

Effervescing and Effacing
Constance Goodman (1917-2013)
Joseph Goodman (1918-2014)

1. Connie

My Joseph and I were married in 1952.
We met in New Haven.
I know, Pooh. Your wedding was the day after your birthday.

When my Joseph and I were children, there were
Civil War veterans marching in the parade.
Yes, Pooh. Manhattan was so different then.

My Joseph and his friend Warren worked
with the Quakers in Mexico during the war.
Conscientious objectors, and your Joseph got himself shot anyway.

I told my Joseph about volunteering in Appalachia
and the woman with a sprouted potato for a tampon.
Oh right, Pooh. You had a devil of a time extracting it.

At that party at the Gregorys', Zaturenska found out I was
a nurse and said, "How useful."
Oh yes, Pooh. She could be terribly rude.

When he had a Fulbright to study composition in Venice,
my Joseph had dinner at Peggy Guggenheim's.
I know, Pooh. He taught music at Queens College, just like me.

I think you would have liked
my Joseph very much, Joe.
Yes, my dear. I think so.

2. Joe

I am blinded by the glare from the light
through the sheer curtains off the glossy paper
on the table, next to this year's red agenda

and a Trollope novel. My head is bathed in light
and I must have an ethereal quality myself
when you say *You look familiar, but I don't*

know why you're here at four o'clock in
the morning. Did you come on horseback?
The glossy paper is the catalogue from Bed Bath

& Beyond, but out of the corner of my eye
through the glare, it says Death & Beyond.
I am seeing the light, but there is no tunnel

end from which it streams. And you,
you are already so much further on
your journey to Aphasia than I.

Amaranthine Days
Jeanne Manna Feiman (1936-2014)
Richard Alan Cowan, Sr. (1937-2014)

Prologue

See Dick and Jeanne meet at Syracuse. They
played house on Falcon Avenue. They had
fun. See Dick and Jeanne have three children: R.

the dog, J. the cat, and R. the teddy
bear. See Dick and Jeanne have a smashing time.
Smash, glass, smash! See Dick and Jeanne separate

in '74 and lead parallel
lives, twenty-three miles apart, for forty
years in the comforting Taconic trees.

I

*Intubate, sino-nasal, metastatic,
pulmonary embolism, DNR—*
Terms and Conditions we sought not to know that

fall. The worst was *cremains*, the ashes. She said
it so matter-of-factly—death-trafficker—
like it was *frog* or *spatula*, the parlance

of her trade. Ashes mostly of the cardboard
box his body was in, not ashes of his
consciousness. But I pushed it out of my mind

with a new word my father had recently
taught us: *bract*—modified leaf with an axil
flower cluster, as on an amaranth, the

imaginary flower that never fades.
I hope my mother dies tonight, I had said
walking once more from Sloan-Kettering to the

6 train, *such suffering*. We had said goodbye
for a week, so it was now shadow time. Dad,
though, never knew what hit him—eighteen days in

the ICU, an operation gone wrong.
Strange to say goodbye to someone so many
times and then get cheated out of the last one.

Jeanne d'Arc had studied graphic design and
Richard the Lion-Hearted forestry then
a half-year as a mountain fire lookout and

a switch to classical philosophy. But
in the library he built no copy of
Plutarch's *Parallel Lives*—twenty-three pairs of

biographies, famous figures arranged in
tandem to illuminate their virtues or
failings—and no account of Jeanne and Dick. Now

they lived *pluperfect lives*, formed by *had* + the
past participle. Lives in the pluperfect,
parallel or not, explain actions prior

to some point that has now passed: *He had died on
All Souls' Day. And she twenty-three days later,
the Monday before Thanksgiving.* Mom buried

at Sleepy Hollow Cemetery, at the
foot of Janis, her best friend from the second
grade. No Washington Irving tale of fear, just

base realism. *We're inhuming her*, I thought,
which sounds like enhuman, not dehuman, unmask
someone so generously and torturedly

wrought. We scattered Dad's ashes toward the end of
the North Fork, at his childhood pond, walking for
a long way to the pristine spot—a blend of

water, sand, trees, and gorgeous ambivalent
sky—but shallow and, instead of dispersing,
the ashes settled on the bottom of the

pond, a cloud of him, spectral and uncanny.
Their bodies don't exist; they dissolve, their minds
—fecund, fragile, free—don't pulse. Not sure their souls

do since both ceased to believe long ago. I
can't feel them very clearly. Maybe that's some-
thing to come later. Maybe they'll touch me, like

the streetlights that I make go out, make themselves
manifest at different points in my life.

II

In winter, in *Grumpy Old Men*, Jack Lemmon has

a heart attack and the camera cuts to him
on a ventilator and I see back to my
father machine-breathing and my mother being

wheeled up to his bedside to say goodbye, with a
huge tumor in her forehead, a smeared flesh tennis
ball. Days numbered. We only number days at the

beginning and the end. Leave the television,
sit down on the toilet with underwear around
ankles, and weep in the dark. There is the thinking

in images—*imagical thinking*. Not night-
mares exactly. Sleep images. Of my father
with forty extra pounds of fluid in him, his

arms spread in an inverted U. Punctures open-
ing, gruesome drains, surreality. Finally
turning off the ventilator like a blood sluice,

like watching an HD TV fade to black and
white. There is guilt for not being more caring to
people whose parents died before mine, the difference

between sympathy and empathy clearer now.
There is nonlinearity. There is *Dad at
Northern Westchester and Mom at Sloan. I can just

drop by each and visit on my way to work*, but
there will be no calling on them. There is joking
that I would never forgive him for making me

read *Misty*, a horse book for girls, but that spring, we
went to Chincoteague to see the wild horses, two
herds—one managed, one not; one that has cowboys and

doctors to check on it, one that lets nature take
its course, just as we have all taken ours. We had
all been so close, laughing and crying and holding,

even singing, but then, after all the rituals
were over, in the wake of the wakes, we were all
so distant, unsure what this misty new constell-

ation is, missing its two focal points, with such
gravitational pull. Stars' light takes so long to
reach us that, even if we know they don't exist

anymore, we can still pretend space-time isn't
warped. Figures of coursing horses and avenue
falcons, of woman warriors and kings. See Dick.

See Jeanne. There! There they had been! So I took two things
from his house: a tie I bought him in Edinburgh,
of the tartan of the Colquohon clan, from whom we

are descended, and a framed picture I took in
Shigatse, of a solar-powered teapot monks
fabricated. When I came back from that trip, he

asked to keep that shot, the one of the Tibetan
teapot, the fascination of invention, of
hand-tooled ingenuity. I stared at his rough

smooth hands as he held up the photo, smiling. Mom
left me her mother's ring: my brother and sister
the sapphires flanking me. I had stared at it on

her meticulously moisturized hands all my
life, special because I was the diamond, unsure
I would have my older siblings at my sides through

the smashing times, feeling her stroke my head sitting
on the floor while she talked on the phone with Janis.

Epilogue

Sunday evenings like this, they are extra

dead. They're never going to not be, right?
All weaker and stronger now. Thinking of
them together, a new experience,

but I can't bring myself to talk to them,
as some do. There is relentless constance
in absence. Ten minutes here or there, ten

minutes of life, to catch my breath, would be
perhaps do-able, the subway ads for
elder care facilities assuring

me that they're going to be fine, that they're
in good hands, that they're going to be well
taken care of. Will I ever again

experience the same happiness? I
must. Because now I can do anything
I want, it doesn't matter, a weird feel-

ing of liberation, I can commit
murder, go to prison, be homeless, crowned,
canonized, an actor, a Wall Street guy,

the obligation to be the best of
who they were dissipated. I'm free to
die without them losing a child, which is

supposedly the worst kind of death. Worlds
look different. Did I get reading glasses
so that I could look over them at things,

at people, at ideas, like my dad
looked at us? To read the world. Looking at
twenty-three days, twenty-three years, twenty-

three miles, twenty-three pairs of lives. How does
one re-establish equilibrium
with a prime number? And how will I free

myself, free any of us—you or me,
our children, their children—from the crushing
awareness of time?

Photo credit: Ada Cowan

Robert Cowan is a literature professor and dean at the City University of New York. He's also the author of *The Indo-German Identification: Reconciling South Asian Origins and European Destinies, 1765-1885* (Camden House, 2010) and *Teaching Double Negatives: Disadvantage and Dissent at Community College* (Peter Lang, 2018). This is his first collection of poetry.

Paloma Press
Poetry+Prose
Est. 2016

Established in 2016, PALOMA PRESS is an independent literary press publishing poetry, prose, and limited edition books. Titles include *BLUE* by Wesley St. Jo & Remé Grefalda (officially launched at The Library of Congress in September 2017), and *MANHATTAN: An Archaeology* by Eileen R. Tabios (which debuted at the 4th Filipino American International Book Festival at the San Francisco Public Library).

We believe in the power of the literary arts, how it can create empathy, bridge divides, change the world. To this end, we have released fundraising chapbooks such as *MARAWI*, in support of relief efforts in the Southern Philippines; and *AFTER IRMA AFTER HARVEY*, in support of hurricane-displaced animals in Texas, Florida and Puerto Rico. As part of the San Francisco Litquake Festival, we proudly curated the wildly successful literary reading, "THREE SHEETS TO THE WIND," and raised money for the Napa Valley Community Disaster Relief Fund.